Preparing an
Episcopal
Funeral

Rob Boulter

with Rev. Kenneth Koehler

Morehouse Publishing

NEW YORK · HARRISBURG · DENVER

Morehouse Publishing
   a division of Church Publishing Incorporated
Editorial Offices:
4775 Lingleston Rd.
Harrisburg, PA 17112

To order additional copies
   call: 1-800-672-1789
   or visit: www.Cokesbury.com

Cover Design: Laurie Westhafer

"Honoring Wishes for End-of-Life Care" copyright Dianne L. Josephson; "After Loss—Putting the Pieces Back Together" and "Seven Tips about What to Say and Do to Comfort Others" copyright Steven V. Malec; all are used with permission of the authors.

Scripture quotations used within are from The Book of Common Prayer and the *New Revised Standard Version* Bible. *The New Revised Standard Version Bible* © 1989 by the Division of Christian Education of the National Council of Churches of Christ in the USA. Used by permission.

Printed in the United States of America

ISBN 978-0-8192-2916-8

A valuable resource for the most poignant of times, you will find resources here to care for the grieving with pastoral insight and the power of finely crafted liturgy. I plan on giving copies of *Preparing an Episcopal Funeral* to newly ordained clergy and pastoral care leaders.

—The Rt. Rev. Mariann Edgar Budde, Bishop,
Episcopal Diocese of Washington DC

Pastors often say that preparing the sermon for Easter Sunday is one of their most difficult tasks. The Resurrection of Christ, with its promise to us, is simultaneously too simple and too vast a topic for that occasion. But we are given the special privilege of sharing that Easter message each time someone in our community dies and enters into Life. *Preparing an Episcopal Funeral* provides practical guidance for the pastor who wishes to share the Easter Gospel during those difficult occasions when people are most hungry to receive it, by both Word and Sacrament, and by their holy companions, pastoral care and administration.

—The Rt. Rev. A. Robert Hirschfeld, Bishop,
Episcopal Diocese of New Hampshire

Short enough to be a realistic and inviting resource for those dealing with the death of a loved one, comprehensive enough to offer insights about every facet of funeral preparation, this handbook expresses with directness and warmth the current pastoral and liturgical practice of Episcopal churches, combining respect for valuable traditions with a thoroughly contemporary orientation.

—The Rev. Martin L. Smith, spiritual guide,
retreat leader and author of books exploring
contemporary spirituality

Rob Boulter's *Preparing an Episcopal Funeral* belongs in every pastor's study, every parish office, every seminary class on pastoral care. It is concise and remarkably clear, combining the pastoral and practical aspects of one of the most delicate and challenging aspects of parish life. How do we celebrate a life, even as we grieve the inevitable passing of a beloved member of our own family or the parish family? How can we, clergy or lay, offer compassionate support to those overwhelmed by grief even as they struggle with decisions great and trivial?

Preparing an Episcopal Funeral is a valuable resource for us all—concise and profoundly useful in preparing for that service of farewell and celebration but also a thought-provoking invitation to reflection for all on the meaning of life and death.

—The Rev. Margaret Guenther, Associate Rector,
St. Columba's Episcopal Church, Washington, DC,
and author of numerous volumes on
spirituality and spiritual direction

Contents

Foreword 6

How to Use this Booklet 8

COPING WITH DEATH

Preparing for Death 9

After Loss—Putting the Pieces Back Together 10

A Counselor Reflects on the Meaning of Funerals 14

Preparing Children for Funerals 16

Honoring Wishes for End-of-Life Care 18

Using Modern Technology and Social Media 21

GUIDELINES FOR PLANNING A FUNERAL

Planning a Funeral or Memorial Service 24

Seven Tips about What to Say and Do to Comfort Others 28

SCRIPTURE READINGS

Introduction 29

Hebrew Scripture 30

Psalms 32

New Testament 39

Gospel Readings 42

MUSIC SUGGESTIONS

Introduction 43

Hymns 44

WORKSHEETS

Vital Information for Survivors and/or Personal Representatives 47

Financial Papers and Records 49

Vital Information for the Funeral Home 51

Funeral Services 53

Vital Information for the Parish Church 55

Foreword

Lord Jesus Christ, by your death you took away the sting of death: Grant to us your servants so to follow in faith where you have led the way, that we may at length fall asleep peacefully in you and wake up in your likeness; for your tender mercies' sake. *Amen.*
—The Book of Common Prayer, Burial II, p. 504

When someone dies, it is important for family and the church community to gather, pray for the soul of the one who has died, and give thanks to God for the gift of that life. We also gather to comfort others who share our feelings of loss and sorrow. At a funeral, grief and gratitude mix together and are held up in prayer to God. But it is important to recognize that funerals are to a great extent for the benefit of the living. Through faith we trust that the one who has died rests now with God. Through faith we believe that the love we feel for the one who has died will never die. It is the loss of their regular presence in our daily lives that makes us sad.

When we gather for a funeral we face death and confront our own mortality. The loss of someone close offers us an opportunity to reflect on their example and consider how we live our own lives. At a time of loss, through God's grace and self-reflection, we pray that *we* might be transformed, just as we know our loved one already has been. Consider this portion of a prayer from the funeral service in The Book of Common Prayer:

O God, whose days are without end, and whose mercies cannot be numbered: Make us, we pray, deeply aware of the shortness and uncertainty of human life; and let your Holy Spirit lead us in holiness and righteousness all our days (p. 504).

A funeral service provides the opportunity for us to come before God in thanksgiving and ask God to fill our lives with meaning and fulfillment. When we gather at a funeral and take measure of the life that we celebrate, we can't help but wonder where we stand in our own mortal existence.

Advance Planning

While it is the responsibility of the clergy to plan the funeral, it is always a great gift when the person who has died has left instructions for their funeral. It is a comfort to know that our loved one has thought about death and has taken the time to write down how she would like to be remembered. Helping to plan a funeral for someone we love can be cathartic and healing; helping to plan for your own funeral can be equally beneficial.

Planning for Yourself

When expressing your wishes for your own funeral, be sure to include information that will be helpful to both your priest and your survivors. We have included forms at the end of the booklet to help you. Include things that your survivors might not know. Do you want to be cremated? Where do you want to be buried? What kind of music do you like? Who should be notified? What are your favorite scripture passages? Do you have a favorite poem or author? Indicate what is most important to you but also leave some things for your family to decide.

You should make your wishes known but also understand that some decisions will be left to your survivors. When someone you love dies, you become painfully aware that much is beyond your control. Working with a priest may be the only thing in which your loved ones have control at that time, so leave some room for them to participate. Planning a funeral is one of the family's and church's final expressions of love and care for the one who has died.

Planning for Someone Else

As you work with your priest to prepare for someone else's funeral, keep in mind that you may need to balance the needs of several people. If you are part of a large family, there will be others who would like to be consulted about the service. Begin by listing the people who will be most affected by this death and then reach out to them as soon as possible. Resist the urge to make all the decisions yourself. Even though there are often time constraints in the planning process, the sooner you have contacted the interested parties the smoother that process will be. If there are tensions in the family, don't avoid them, deal with them directly. Sometimes a death can bring out the worst in a family, but it more often brings out the best. Planning for a funeral can be a profound act of healing for a family if you open lines of communication rather than close them down.

One of the first decisions you will need to make is when and where the service will take place. Although most often conducted at the church, circumstances (and local custom) may mean the service is held elsewhere. Once that decision is made, most others build from there. Have two or three options in mind when speaking with clergy. In the past, the funeral would take place within a few days of the death, but, in reality, this is no longer the norm. I encourage families to leave enough time to make travel arrangements but not so much time that people are left alone with their feelings of grief. Typically one to two weeks from the death is a good time frame. Have a firm commitment from the church concerning the date and time before you share the information with the public.

How to Use this Booklet

This booklet is the culmination of years of experience helping people face the often unfamiliar task of preparing a funeral or memorial service. It is designed to manage the many practical details that go into planning a funeral and to help gather the information that will be of help for the survivors, the funeral home, the cemetery and the church. It is not meant to be a treatise on the history and practice of burial rituals, but rather a practical and pastoral guide with helpful instruction concerning current practices and expectations.

This booklet may be used either by those who have just experienced the death of a loved one or by those who wish to decide in advance about the many details of their own funeral. These advance decisions allow that, when death does occur, the survivors will have a record of the deceased's wishes and will be able to plan the funeral liturgy in a way that respects these wishes.

This booklet has been created to ensure that the practical details connected with planning a funeral are attended to in a way that helps all involved make the funeral an appropriate celebration of the life of the person who has died.

Using the Instruction Forms

At the end of this booklet, there are forms that may be completed, torn out, copied and given to one's relatives, personal representative or attorney, the funeral home and the church to keep on file. The information and instructions on these forms will be helpful for making the funeral plans. It is important to work together with the cemetery, funeral home and church where the funeral will be celebrated before final decisions are made concerning the funeral.

Coping with Death

Preparing for Death

When Death Is Near

When someone faces death or is critically ill, family members should immediately contact that person's church. A priest or lay pastoral minister can provide comfort for the person who is dying as well as for the family. Don't wait until death is imminent to contact the church. There are several options for ministration to the sick in the Episcopal tradition including the "Laying on of Hands for Healing" and "Anointing of the Sick." It is usually fairly easy to arrange for a priest to visit and offer Holy Communion when someone is too sick to come to church. Participation in these rites encourages the sick or dying person to experience the healing presence of Christ, whose resurrection offers hope for a new life beyond suffering and death.

Be certain to share with all loved ones as well as clergy the dying person's wishes for the funeral celebration, for example, by using the forms found on pages 47-56 of this booklet—if they have been filled out in advance. Review whether prior arrangements might have been made for someone to make decisions on the sick person's behalf (for example, through a durable power of attorney or a living will), for organ donation, for the burial plot, vault, marker or niche for cremated remains in a cemetery or for prepaid funeral plans.

When Death Occurs

When a loved one dies, the family should call the person's church as soon as possible. Most churches have an on-call system that will allow you to reach a priest and deacon when you need one. The sacrament of the "Anointing of the Sick" is for the living; therefore, the priest does not, typically, anoint the deceased person (but could, especially if the priest arrives a short time after the moment of death). Most often the priest/deacons will pray with the family in the presence of the body for the eternal salvation of the deceased and for the consolation of those who are gathered.

If no choice of a cemetery and funeral home has been made, the hospital, nursing home or facility where the death took place will assist the family or responsible person to choose and contact a funeral home. Should the death take place at home, the family should consult any available records indicating the deceased's wishes or any prior arrangements with a funeral home. Otherwise, they should choose a funeral home whose reputation they trust. If a funeral home has already been chosen, then it will be necessary to contact them immediately. There is a form at the end of the booklet (p. 51) to gather the information that the funeral home would normally request.

After Loss—Putting the Pieces Back Together

by Steven V. Malec

Life and death are partners. At some point, all of us will face death: our own as well as those we love. To lose a loved one through death always causes changes for us and for our lives. Life is about change. Sometimes it is painful. Sometimes it is beautiful. Many times it can be both.

After the overwhelming loss of a loved one, it feels like your heart—and your entire world—is completely shattered into pieces. No one asks for life to change this way, but it does. We have no control over death, but we do have control over how we respond to death. How we respond is what counts. After a loss, we find out who we are as we go about putting the pieces of ourselves and our lives back together.

The First Piece: Recognize the Loss

If grief is to be healed, it must be identified, acknowledged, felt and expressed. Grief only destroys us when we deny it or refuse to deal with it. Admit and honor your feelings of loss. The psychologist and spiritual writer Henri Nouwen counsels that "The only feelings that do not heal are the ones you hide." Therefore, the only cure for grief is to grieve. It is as simple and as difficult as that.

To begin grieving, you need to accept the full reality of your loss—in both the big and all the little ways. The primary loss is that of your loved one; however, there are always a host of other losses as well. You need to identify all the losses that the death of your loved one involves. Make a list and identify all your losses so you know exactly what you are dealing with.

The Second Piece: Express the Loss

Initially, a very important step in the healing process is to tell and retell the story of your loss, with all of its pain. We need to experience the pain and express it in order to heal. Pain and emotional feelings are essential ingredients in the healing process.

Sharing your loss helps to ease that pain. You can share your loss by talking, writing, crying and praying. Grief is not a problem that we fix or solve, but an experience that we must embrace and express in order to heal.

Grieving is not something that must be done alone either. Ask for help from your family, friends, church and professional agencies. Don't always wait for others to read your mind and offer help. Make a list of what you need and be willing to accept the help that others offer. Be gentle and patient with yourself and realistic with what you can and simply cannot do at this time. Keep in touch with supportive friends or others who have been in a similar situation. Think about attending a support group.

The Third Piece: Learn about Grief

Grief is the normal, natural and appropriate response to the loss of a loved one. It is essential for the healing process. You are not going crazy; you are grieving. You work through the loss of a loved one by moving from the deep pain, intense sorrow and distressing regret to healing, inner peace and even joy.

It helps to learn all you can about the grief process. Read literature on grief and loss and watch the newspaper for articles about grief. Check with your church for support and resources. Look up websites that have information on grief. Get on the mailing list for bereavement care newsletters from your cemetery, funeral home and area hospice.

The Fourth Piece: Face Your Loss

As you grieve, you are going to hurt. Grieving means living with pain. But that pain is the sign that you loved someone and someone loved you. You will always miss them and long to hear their voice one more time and that is okay. You cannot heal what you do not allow yourself to feel. Over time, each day will get a little better.

Each person's experience of loss is unique, but there are also common elements of grief. There is no right or wrong way to grieve, no orderly stages of progression. There are, however, healthy and unhealthy ways to cope with your grief.

Some healthy ways of coping include: talking about your loss with family, friends and others, writing in a journal, prayer, visiting the grave, looking at photos, honoring your feelings and taking good care of yourself physically and spiritually.

Doing these things often brings lots of tears. For both women and men, crying is a natural response to sorrow and can be extremely healing. Crying supports the immune system. Scientists have discovered that tears of sadness are chemically different from tears of joy. Crying these tears of sorrow flushes out depressants from the body.

You must also learn how to deal with the pain of your grief. The death of a loved one is the greatest of hurts that you will ever endure, and healing is never easy. Grieving takes courage, patience, endurance and faith. And though grieving is healthy and necessary, still it takes a huge toll on your body, mind and soul. So make sure to get proper rest, nutrition and exercise.

The Fifth Piece: Work through Your Grief

Grief has many different names and faces. When grieving a loss, it is normal to experience any of the following: shock/disbelief/numbness; loneliness/emptiness; fear/anxiety; anger/hostility; deep sadness/situational depression; a lack of purpose; a lack of energy; inability to concentrate; change in eating habits; change in sleeping habits; guilt/regret/relief; searching; envy of others; a strengthening or weakening of faith; acceptance/survival/healing.

Be determined to take time, notice and work through your grief even if others may want to hurry you through it. The funeral and burial may be finished in a week, but grieving goes on for a much longer time. The initial grief reactions of shock and disbelief are not the most painful or enduring ones. The five main grief reactions that usually remain the longest are anger, guilt, fear, sadness and loneliness. As you work through your grief, these acute grief reactions often lessen in intensity and soften. But you will have feelings of grief and will keep having them until you no longer need to.

There comes a time in your grief process when you will need to press through your emotions and grief reactions. Do not allow the "whys," the guilt or the regret to paralyze you in your grieving. If you do become stuck in your grief or if there is an issue that you cannot resolve, you may want to seek professional help. Also, let your faith help to heal you—in prayer give these unresolved areas to God as a seed and you will discover that God will bring you a harvest.

The Sixth Piece: Manage Your Loss

There is no easy way to bypass the experience of grief when a loved one dies. You must learn to manage your loss and not have your loss manage you. Bad things do happen to good people. You are still fragile, yet strong. Your heart is shattered, your bones ache and there are knots in your stomach.

Time alone does not heal all wounds, but rather what you do with your time does. Your heart is deeply wounded, and it will take time and hard work for healing to occur. While there is no set time schedule for the grief process, research shows that most grief reactions will be experienced and healed within 2-4 years for an anticipated loss and 4-7 years for a sudden loss. Although we usually want to know how long our grief will last, it is better to ask how willing are we to accept the reality of pain and truly work toward healing it.

Gradually, you will not only reclaim aspects of your old life but also add new ones, too. You will never really "get over it," but you can get through it. Through grieving, "moving on" is really moving back to former activities that you used to do and enjoy—dining out, going to the movies, doing hobbies, shopping, singing in church, among others.

We never really "let go" of our loved ones, but we do loosen our grip a little bit and let go of some of the pain. They are still a part of you and

always will be! Take time to make a little connection with them every day.

The Seventh Piece: Hope for Healing

At the root of our faith is an unshakeable hope. Death is not the end. We believe that with Christ, there is life after death—"for your faithful people life has changed, not ended" (Preface of Christian Death, 1). Knowing and experiencing this makes our grief much different. It may not be any easier, but it is different.

We are like the Israelites who, when faced with the destruction of Jerusalem and its temple, did not despair but dared to hope and cried out in their grief: "My soul is bereft of peace; I have forgotten what happiness is. My soul continually thinks of my affliction and is bowed down within me. Yet I still dare to hope when I remember this: the steadfast love of the Lord never ceases, his mercies never come to an end" (Lamentations 3:17, 20-22).

We too dare to hope in the Lord. When a loved one dies, we grieve their loss. Christians grieve like everyone else, but we also grieve with faith and look to the crucified and risen Jesus for our hope. St. Paul encourages us to trust in the power of Christ's resurrection: "We do not want you to be uninformed, brothers and sisters, about those who have died so that you may not grieve as others who have no hope. For since we believe that Jesus died and rose again even so, through Jesus, God will bring with him those who have died" (1 Thessalonians 4:13-14).

There is life after death for your loved one. There is also life after loss for you! After the death of a loved one, your life has been changed because of your loss. Over time, your grief will change, too. It will soften. You will not always feel as you do at this moment.

But just because your life has changed, this doesn't mean it is ruined. There is hope and healing. First you must allow yourself to feel the pain of loss and grief. Then in time and with hard work, the good days will begin to outnumber the bad days.

Let faith be your consolation and eternal life your hope. Jesus can help you heal if you invite him into the process. Through Jesus' suffering and death, we find hope and healing. It is an unrealistic expectation, however, to think that healing will restore your life back exactly the way it was before your loss. There is no full recovery. Some part of your loss may remain unrecovered for the rest of your life.

This doesn't mean that you cannot have peace and joy within you. Healing involves making peace with your life and even finding joy again. There is always loss before gain. Through this healing process, you will emerge a new person—stronger, more compassionate, more understanding and loving, with a life full of renewed meaning, purpose and love.

Putting the Pieces Back Together

Although this life has to end, love doesn't. A heart can be broken; but it still keeps beating. You can feel shattered, but you can put the pieces together again. Healing is a daily journey and a constant choice to go on and to look forward. Healing comes not from the forgetting, but from the remembering. Piece by piece, you will be healing.

May you experience the peace of Jesus Christ, which is beyond all understanding, as you journey through your loss to heal and anticipate your joyful reunion with all your loved ones.

About the Author

Steven V. Malec, BBA, NCBF is a national speaker and Director of Bereavement Ministry for the Catholic Cemeteries Association in the Diocese of Cleveland, Ohio.

A Counselor Reflects on the Meaning of Funerals

by Alan D. Wolfelt, Ph.D.

For thousands of years, funerals have been a means of expressing our beliefs, thoughts and feelings about the death of someone we love. The funeral ceremony…

❖ helps us acknowledge that someone we love has died.

❖ helps us remember the person who died and encourages us to share those memories with others.

❖ offers a time and place for us to talk about the life and death of the person who died.

❖ provides a social support system for us and other friends and family members.

❖ allows us to search for the meaning of life and death in the context of our faith.

❖ offers continuity and hope for the living.

One of the most important gifts of planning a meaningful funeral is that it helps family and friends to focus their thoughts and feelings on something positive. The funeral encourages them to think about the person who has died and to explore the meaning of that person's life and the ways in which she touched the lives of others. It is also a time and place for them to reaffirm their faith in new life after death.

The remembering, deciding and reflecting that takes place in the planning of the service are often an important part of the process of grief and mourning. And ultimately, this process of contemplation and discovery creates a memorable and moving funeral experience for all who attend.

Some time ago I created this layered triangle graphic to capture my philosophy of the Hierarchy of Purposes of the Funeral. Let's look at each layer in turn:

Reality

When someone we love dies, we are faced with acknowledging a difficult reality. It is hard to truly accept the finality of death, but the funeral helps us begin to do so. At first we accept it with our heads, and only over time do we come to accept it with our hearts.

Recall

Funerals help us begin to convert our relationship with the person who died from one of presence to one of memory. When we come together to share our memories, we learn things we didn't know and we see how the person's life touched others.

Support

Funerals are social gatherings that bring together people who cared about the person who died. This reason for having funerals is especially

Transcendence

Meaning

Expression

Support

Recall

Reality

important to remember if the person who died liked to say, "I don't want a funeral. Don't go to any trouble." Funerals are in *remembrance* of the person who died, but they are *for* the living. Those who loved the person who died need and benefit from having a special time to support one another in their grief.

Expression

So many thoughts and feelings fill our minds and our hearts when someone we love dies. Collectively, these thoughts and feelings are what we mean by the term "grief." In other words, grief is what's inside us. When we *express* our grief—by crying, talking to others, sharing memories, taking part in a funeral ceremony— we are mourning. Mourning is grief communicated outwardly. When we grieve but do not mourn, our sadness can feel unbearable and our many other emotions can fester inside of us. Mourning helps us begin to heal. The funeral is an essential time for mourning.

Meaning

Did the person I love have a good life? What is life, anyway? There are no simple explanations, but the funeral gives us a time and a place to hold the questions in our hearts and begin to find our way to answers that give us peace.

Transcendence

Funerals have a way of getting us to wake up— to think about what we truly care about and how we want to spend our precious remaining days. Ultimately, funerals help us embrace the wonder of life and death and remind us to live deeply, with joy and love.

Planning a Funeral is a Privilege

As you consider the funeral, try to remember that planning a funeral is not a burden, but a privilege. Think of the funeral as a gift to the person who died as well as his friends and family. It is a chance for all to think about and express the value of the life that was lived. It is also a chance to say goodbye.

This is not to deny the need of friends and family members to mourn and to embrace painful feelings of grief in the coming days. They may feel deep sadness as they plan this funeral and begin to acknowledge the reality of the death. But when all is said and done, all those involved in planning the funeral also feel deep satisfaction that they have helped plan a meaningful tribute. And those who loved the person who died begin to work their way from the bottom of the pyramid—acknowledging the reality of the death—to the top.

Planning and attending a meaningful funeral can have a lasting and profoundly important impact on the lives of so many people. Tapping into the power of ceremony assists them on their journey to transcendence.

About the Author

Alan D. Wolfelt, Ph.D., is a respected author and educator on the topic of grief. He believes that meaningful funeral experiences help families and friends support one another, embrace their feelings, and embark on the journey to healing and transcendence. Recipient of the Association of Death Education and Counseling's Death Educator Award, Dr. Wolfelt presents workshops across the world and teaches training courses at the Center for Loss and Life Transition in Fort Collins, Colorado, where he serves as Director. He is also the author of many bestselling books, including Understanding Your Grief, The Mourner's Book of Hope *and* Creating Meaningful Funeral Ceremonies. *For more information, visit www.centerforloss.com.*

Preparing Children for Funerals
by Rev. Kenneth Koehler

Often people want to "protect" children from the harsh reality of a death. Yet the child is part of the family for whom death causes a major change in their lives. So children should be drawn into discussions regarding the death and the funeral planning. Adults often resist allowing children into this conversation because adults fear not being able to answer children's questions. But experts recommend this involvement to help both adults and children with their grieving.

Communication about death is easier when a child feels that he or she has our permission to talk about a subject often not talked about, especially with children. We must deal with the inescapable fact of death, and so must our children. To help them, let them know that it is okay to talk about it. In fact, any discussion with the children will also aid adults in their own grief process.

Death should be explained to a child as simply and directly as possible by someone very close. Listen carefully to the child and consider the child's feelings about this particular death or about death in general. Adults need to realize that the child's understanding of death always depends upon his or her age, maturity and intelligence.

Children from ages three to five usually know very little, if anything, about death. But since they are very curious, they can have many questions that should be answered as simply, directly and truthfully as possible, especially without suggesting that death is reversible or has not really happened.

Children from ages five to nine have begun to understand that death is final, and their questions can often be harder to answer. But again, direct and truthful answers will help them confront the reality of death and cope with their own grief.

Older children, ten through the teenage years, might recognize death's inevitability and also realize it could happen to them. Anger and guilt feelings can also occur in relation to a death, especially one within their family, friends or peer group. It is important to communicate that they were in no way responsible for the death.

When a death occurs, the children should be given the news in a way that gives them time to ask questions and includes them in the emotional experience of the whole family. They are an important part of the family and should be included when the family celebrates and grieves together.

Whether or not a particular child should be included in the funeral depends upon the child and the situation. If he or she is asking questions about the death, then they are probably old enough to be present at all the events of the funeral and reception. If the child is old enough to understand and wants to participate, being included may help accept the reality of death and offer a way to express grief in the company of family and friends. If a child prefers not to attend the funeral, it is not wise for the child to be coerced or made to feel guilty.

If a child is to attend a funeral, preparation should be given beforehand about what will be seen and heard before, during and after the service. Children often feel unsure about their social skills and have difficulty trying to figure out what to say and do. Help the child understand that on such sad occasions, no one ever has just the right words of consolation for the survivors. Let the child know that at the funeral people will also be expressing their sorrow in various ways and many will be crying, which is a very appropriate expression of sadness and grief when a loved one dies.

If children need more assistance in answering their questions, parishes, funeral directors or cemeteries often have bereavement resources that can be used to help children understand and cope with their experience of death. Remember that not only for adults but also for children, healing will take time and continuing support to help them through the grieving process.

About the Author

Rev. Kenneth Koehler has been a clergyperson for over 25 years and a priest for nearly 40. He has served two Denver parishes, where he has conducted 35-40 funerals per year. Rev. Koehler currently serves as Pastor of St. Mark's Catholic Church in Westminster, Colorado.

Honoring Wishes for End-of-Life Care
by Dianne L. Josephson

Human Life Is Sacred

The joy of a new life coming into the world is openly discussed and celebrated, yet we often shun the "uncomfortable" topic of death. Death, however, when openly embraced as a natural part of the life continuum, can be one of the most beautiful and spiritual moments of our lives.

Jesus presented us with the finest model of how to confront death with dignity, fortitude and hope. Throughout his life, he taught us how to understand death in the context of love, compassion, forgiveness, peace and the assurance of eternal life. As followers of Christ, we are called upon to imitate Christ when we comfort the sick and the dying, walk with those who are grieving, embrace our own mortality and prepare for our journey home to God. With advance planning, we validate life and accept the inevitability of death.

Needs of the Dying

When we fully acknowledge our mortality and embrace death, we also take care of the common needs that confront us at the end of life. These encompass all aspects of our legacy, including making financial plans, drawing up a will to provide for those we leave behind, writing advance directives to help ease the burden on loved ones when we can no longer address our own care and providing a durable power of attorney to ensure that our wishes are followed in the event that we are too incapacitated to make our own medical decisions.

Advance Directives and Durable Power of Attorney

Advance directives include a living will (or medical directive) and a durable power of attorney for health care (or healthcare proxy). When writing advance directives, people often choose a combination of these. Since laws vary from state to state regarding advance directives, it is wise to contact an estate attorney to determine specifics for a particular state. Costs vary for such services, especially when dealing with a complex estate. The cost, however, may be worth it to avoid legal battles for survivors.

Without an advance directive, some of the hardest and most important decisions of a person's life can be left entirely in the hands of medical professionals, family members or the state. An advance directive is legal in every state, and most hospitals will allow a person to keep a copy of an advance directive on file with them. Having an advance directive on file can help ease a person's fear about what will happen once admitted to a hospital for treatment or end-of-life care.

Advance directives make it possible to indicate ahead of time what medical procedures a person does or does not want. They often include decisions about pain control, breathing machines, intravenous or gastric delivery of medications, fluids and nutrients, cardiopulmonary resuscitation and organ donation. They also assist family members in making very difficult decisions while ensuring that a person's expectations are followed when these might be different or opposed to those of family members.

A durable power of attorney for health care, which is different from a regular power of attorney, gives another person the power to make healthcare decisions for us. In it, we designate someone to make medical decisions for us if we become too ill or unable to make them. Healthcare providers and legal advisors encourage that, regardless of a person's health status or age, one have a living will and, more importantly, a durable power of attorney for health care.

Death with Dignity

When we come to terms with the inevitability of our own death, then it is important to be as detailed as possible regarding the circumstance of our death. We all want to die with dignity but it is up to us to attend to the details.

We are the only ones who can honestly make choices regarding our own end-of-life care. It is important to thoroughly think through what we want and don't want, discuss these desires with trusted loved ones or friends and then write them down in a legal document, as described above. It is our life and we need to state clearly the way we want to die.

In doing these things, we also show our love for family by relieving them of the burden of decision making. It is never too early to discuss and make these decisions. We must not wait until a health crisis occurs.

Each one of us needs to address questions such as:

❖ What are my fears about dying?
❖ What are my fears about losing control of my mental and bodily functions?
❖ If I were to become very ill (cancer, disabling stroke, unconscious) what type of medical care and treatment would I want/not want?
❖ Would I want to be kept comfortable with pain control or would I prefer to be kept alive as long as possible on machines?
❖ What are my feelings about pain management?
❖ Do I want to remain alert, even if it means I have some degree of pain, or would I prefer to be totally free of pain, regardless of my state of consciousness?
❖ If I could no longer swallow, would I want feeding tubes and intravenous supplements?
❖ Would I want my life prolonged by the technology of machines if I could no longer think for myself, become comatose or terminally ill and near death?
❖ Who would I want to take care of me (family, health professionals)?
❖ Where do I want to die (at home with hospice care, in a hospital or a long-term care facility)?
❖ Who do I want to make decisions for me?
❖ Do I want to donate my organs?
❖ Do I want an autopsy?
❖ What do I want for the final disposition of my body (burial, cremation, other)?
❖ What kind of funeral service do I want?
❖ How do I want to be remembered?

Once we have thoroughly and honestly considered and answered these questions, it is time to act on them. When steadfast regarding our personal beliefs and desires, then only can we approach a spouse, parent, child or other trusted individual about what is best for us. The choice is ours.

By facing death, and preparing for it physically, emotionally and spiritually, we can live out our days in peace. As followers of Jesus Christ, we give testimony to his life and death and find our hope by trusting in his resurrection. Then, with a sense of peace, we are able to live fully, even while we are dying, because we realize the truth of the prayer of St. Francis of Assisi, "that it is in dying that we are born to eternal life."

Involving the Family, the Funeral Home, the Cemetery and the Parish Church

When the death of a loved one has occurred, the wishes of the deceased regarding the funeral plans should be reviewed, using, for example, the forms found at the end of this booklet if they have been prepared in advance (pp. 47-56).

After connecting with your priest, the funeral home and the cemetery will be contacted. A date, time and place for both the funeral liturgy and the burial need to be established in collaboration with the parish, the cemetery and the mortuary.

Once the date for the funeral and final disposition of the body is set, this then gives the parties time to carry out their tasks. The parish can schedule the church for the funeral, arrange for musicians, prepare for a reception, etc. The mortuary will prepare the body for the funeral and for the final disposition. The cemetery can prepare the plot or mausoleum or the niche for the cremated remains. Meanwhile, the family is given time to notify their relatives and friends and make travel arrangements if necessary.

When making arrangements with the parish staff or planning team, there will be many decisions to make about the funeral liturgy. The parish is primarily responsible for scheduling and planning the liturgy, which includes such things as the selection of scripture readings and designation of readers, the selection of music and musicians, the eulogist and many other

details about the ceremony. The parish, in turn, gives all that information to the funeral home after the planning session. The form in this booklet for the parish church (p. 55) will help to keep track of the many details that must be considered for celebrating the funeral liturgy.

When making arrangements with the cemetery, there will be important decisions about the final disposition of the body. Will the burial be in the ground in a plot and will there need to be a vault (a concrete form surrounding the casket), or will it be above ground in a mausoleum or crypt? If the body is to be cremated, will the cremated remains be buried in the ground or put in a special niche (a columbarium)? What will the burial marker or monument be?

When making arrangements with the mortuary, there will be decisions about the casket, obituary notices, prayer or memory cards, ushers, etc. The form in this booklet for the mortuary (p. 51) will be helpful for gathering most of the information that the mortuary will want to have.

After these initial planning sessions, the parish, the mortuary and the cemetery can begin their work. As the planning process unfolds, however, the family or persons responsible for planning the funeral should stay in contact with the parish, the mortuary and the cemetery to make sure that everything is proceeding smoothly and any problems that arise can be quickly resolved.

About the Author

Dianne L. Josephson, RN, MSN is an author, educator, consultant and Director of the Healing After Loss Ministry at St. Pius X Parish, El Paso, TX.

Using Modern Technology and Social Media

by Rev. Kenneth Koehler with Amy Sander Montanez and Dirk deVries

Today's computer technology—coupled with social media like Facebook, Twitter and blogging—makes it easy and quick to communicate important information regarding any parish matter, including the death of a parishioner. How often have we heard: "I didn't know she passed away!" or "The funeral was *when?* Nobody told me!" The question is: How can we get the information to as many people as possible so that the right people know what they need to know, quickly and efficiently?

Social media and our connection to the world through our computers offer many useful ways to communicate such information. Most cell phones now have texting and email capabilities, so word can spread quickly and efficiently. Most people have at least minimal Internet skills; many use Facebook and check it frequently. The notice about a death or a funeral can thus be shared very quickly.

Many churches themselves have the technology and staff to create and maintain their own Facebook pages, email lists and blogs; any and all of these can be effective ways to communicate the announcement of a death and the funeral arrangements to all members of the parish.

Ideally, your parish will already have established *clear policies* regarding the announcement of deaths and the details of funeral arrangements, *and* these policies will have been communicated so everyone in the parish knows what to expect, including how the announcement is made, what to communicate, when to say it and to whom. If your parish is large enough to have a communications committee or department, they would be the natural ones to work out this policy and make sure all in the parish are aware of it. If you don't have one, now's the time to develop one!

In regard to funerals, as the family of the deceased, you will have input about *what* is to be communicated, as well as *when*, *how* and *to whom*. Some families may be sensitive about some unusual circumstances that need to be considered before moving ahead. But again, what is your parish's established policy? In some parishes, it's assumed that families will be contacted first and allowed to decide what means of communicating will be used, though there are parishes in which it's understood some announcements may be made without consulting the family. Ask your clergy person to help you understand the church's policy.

In regard to specifics about the funeral, if you do not have the money to place a notice in the newspaper, you could choose Internet options to communicate these details. Many funeral homes also provide their own Web page to communicate details of funerals and the contact information for families. That same Web page will often offer a place for people to leave their condolences and prayers or to share meaningful memories or experiences they had with the deceased.

In the hours following a death, most often you will contact one of the priests or a parish minister. There is usually a phone number on the office's phone answering menu that will put you in touch with the correct person. The parish staff will want to make a personal contact to arrange a one-on-one visit with you, not only to comfort, but also to begin the process of planning for the funeral.

Most importantly, the parish will want to hold as a priority face-to-face communication with the family of the deceased before any action is taken. Despite the ease and advantages of today's electronic and social media options, there is no substitute for hugs, shared tears and the offer of practical, hands-on help. Don't allow electronic options (which, lacking the tone of voice, the personal touch, the look on the face, etc. can be misunderstood or misinterpreted) to take the place of our customary ways of communicating and offering support.

If your parish does not have the technology, ask if a family member or friend has a Facebook, email or blog address you can leave with the parish receptionist; this could be given to those who wish to express their condolences electronically and provide a place where they can periodically check for additional details about the upcoming funeral or memorial service. When you meet with the liturgical planner or priest, you can arrange what you would like to be put in place. The goal: to support both the parish and the family, and to more effectively mobilize your parish community in sharing your grief, offering their support and celebrating the life of a fellow parishioner.

An additional helpful online resource is CaringBridge, which you'll find at *www.caringbridge.org*. This Internet site provides a place to set up a free, personal page when a family member is seriously ill and the prognosis is poor. Once people know that a family has established

a CaringBridge account, friends, family members and parishioners who visit and register at CaringBridge page will be automatically notified when the family has posted anything new to the site, including changes in the patient's physical status, how treatment is proceeding and when (if) the death occurs. Those who respond can, in turn, leave their own messages for the patient and the family. CaringBridge also offers online suggestions for helping both family and friends through the process of death and dying. After the death, CaringBridge can continue to be a place for friends and parishioners to check in on the family to see how they're doing in the process of grieving and healing.

And finally, in today's online world, it's important, as we look ahead to our own potential illness and eventual passing, to include the necessary online information in the forms provided at the end of this book. This includes not only email addresses for online accounts (banks, investments firms, etc.), but also your login name and your password, so that your survivors will be able to communicate regarding your accounts. This has been a major change to how most of us go about our day-to-day business.

To conclude: you and your parish have a great opportunity to make use of the Internet and social media to communicate and to comfort when it comes to serious illness and death in the parish. Never forget, however, that electronic communication can only supplement the personal, not replace it!

About the Authors

Amy Sander Montanez, D.Min, has been a licensed professional counselor, licensed marriage and family therapist, and spiritual director for over 20 years. Her areas of expertise include all aspects of women's issues, leadership during hard times, forgiveness, grief work, healthy relationships, building healthy families and communities, the spiritual journey, healing and the mind–body–spirit connection. Amy is an Episcopalian living in Columbia, South Carolina.

Dirk deVries, MA, MCE, is a former pastor in the Christian Reformed Church and the current Director of Curriculum Development for Morehouse Education Resources, a Division of Church Publishing Incorporated. He is also a speaker in the areas of religious addiction and spiritual abuse, as well as a photographer and regular blogger on matters of faith and spiritual growth.

Guidelines for Planning a Funeral

Planning a Funeral or Memorial Service

A funeral or memorial service offers family, friends and the entire faith community an important opportunity to gather and give thanks to God for the life of someone important to them. The Book of Common Prayer calls this service "The Burial of the Dead," though the local church may have its own customary title for this service. For example, at the churches where I have served, we call the gathering "A Service in Celebration and Thanksgiving for the Life of..." It sounds strange to say that we gather to *celebrate* when someone has died, but the Episcopal Funeral service is truly an *Easter celebration*…a celebration of redemption, of the promise of eternal life in Christ. The opening sentences of the liturgy give voice to our theological understanding of death and the afterlife:

I am Resurrection and I am Life, says
    the Lord.
Whoever has faith in me shall have life,
even though he die.
And everyone who has life,
and has committed himself to me in faith,
shall not die for ever.

As for me, I know that my Redeemer lives
and that at the last he will stand upon
    the earth.
After my awaking, he will raise me up;
and in my body I shall see God.
I myself shall see, and my eyes behold him
who is my friend and not a stranger.

For none of us has life in himself,
and none becomes his own master when
    he dies.

For if we have life, we are alive in the Lord,
and if we die, we die in the Lord.
So, then, whether we live or die,
we are the Lord's possession.

Happy from now on
are those who die in the Lord!
So it is, says the Spirit,
for they rest from their labors.
                    —The Book of Common Prayer,
                                pp. 491-492)

From the first words, spoken or sung, we affirm that in death life is not over; it is changed. "Because Jesus was raised from the dead, we, too, shall be raised" (BCP, p. 507). Although we stress that this time of worship is a celebration, we know it is coupled with loss and grief. "The Burial of the Dead," as outlined in the *BCP*, provides an outlet for the variety of feelings people will need to express.

It is very appropriate that the gathering take place in the church community of the person that has died. During our lifetime, we gather in communities of faith to support and encourage each other to live into our calling as members of the body of Christ. The gathering at the *end* of one's life echoes the gathering that happens at the *beginning* of one's life in Christ—*the service of Holy Baptism*. The Paschal candle will be lit and take a place of prominence in the church to reinforce the commitment we make at baptism as the Christian journey begins. We reaffirm at the end of one's mortal life that the One who made us and called us to serve receives us again after we take our last breath. God creates, Christ calls, the Spirit motivates, and at the end we rest again in the heart of God. We hear this connection to Baptism very clearly in the introduction to the Creed when the officiating priest says "In the assurance of eternal life given at Baptism, let us proclaim our faith." The gathering for the Burial Rite is the ultimate statement of faith in God, in Christ and in the Church.

Please note the page of guidelines offered in the prayer book on page 46, titled *Concerning the Service*.

Prayer for a Vigil

If the family wants to have a calling hours before the funeral, there is a lovely service of Prayers for a Vigil in The Book of Common Prayer (p. 465). While the custom of gathering for a prayer vigil in the church or funeral home is not widespread in the Episcopal tradition, those who practice this rite as a normal part of their grieving process find the time together to be peaceful and healing.

Rite One or Rite Two

The *BCP* provides two versions of the burial service. The Rite One form of the service was taken from The Book of Common Prayer, *1928* and includes Elizabethan English. For example, the opening sentences begin:

> I am the resurrection and the life, saith the Lord;
> he that believeth in me, though he were dead, yet shall he live;
> and whosoever liveth and believeth in me shall never die.

The Rite Two version has a very similar structure but includes language that is closer to current usage. The decision to use Rite One or Rite Two is always made in conjunction with the officiating priest and keeping in mind the norms of the church and the wishes of the person who has died.

What Is the Difference between a Funeral and a Memorial Service?

The difference between a funeral and a memorial service is that when the remains of the person who has died, either a coffin or an urn of ashes are present in the church, the service is called a *funeral*. The distinction, from the church's point of view, is not very important, because in both circumstances we use the same liturgy.

The Bulletin or Service Leaflet

The people who gather for a funeral or memorial service will come from a variety of faith traditions, so prepare a user-friendly, printed bulletin for the service. Those who gather should feel comfortable participating in the service. The Episcopal Church has many traditions and practices that are unfamiliar to others, and providing a clear outline of what to expect with appropriate instruction is an act of hospitality and evangelism. Include the order of service, including all readings, prayers and music.

Giving a Remembrance, Homily or Eulogy

Practices vary in congregations concerning the giving of a remembrance, eulogy, tribute or homily. The Book of Common Prayer states that after the scripture readings "Here there may be a homily by the Celebrant, or a member of the family, or a friend." This is not required, nor is it always permitted (depending on the parish); consult with the clergy in charge. You might think of one or two people who were close to the deceased who might feel comfortable offering a few words of remembrance.

It is important that the family members who have been given the responsibility of planning the service be careful and considerate in their decision about who might speak. The person to offer a remembrance should be comfortable in front of a crowd and able to maintain composure in difficult circumstances. According to The Book of Common Prayer, the remembrances may be offered after the Gospel Reading. Expect there to be some anxiety that comes with speaking in public about a loved one who has died.

Consider limiting the remembrance to 5 minutes (about 500 words). This length allows the opportunity to reflect at some depth about the person who has died but not get into a chronology or biography. One tip for those speaking: select one attribute of the person and highlight it with personal memories and stories. There is no way to encapsulate a life in the midst of an hour-long worship service, nor should we try. A good, concise remembrance sets the tone for the celebration and triggers later conversations and sharing of memories between those who have gathered. (Note that an opportunity for other friends and family members to speak about the person who has died can be scheduled for the reception or other gathering after the service.)

Have remembrances written out in advance. If a speaker has a text in hand and becomes unable to speak, someone else may step forward and offer their words on their behalf. Speaking at the funeral of a loved one presents a unique challenge; advance planning and preparation goes a long way to ensuring a positive experience for the family and for those who have gathered. If more than one person will speak, invite them to share their remarks with one another *before* the day of the service so that the remembrances they offer have variety and continuity.

Holy Communion

There is a provision in the funeral rite for the inclusion of the Eucharist (strongly recommended!), though the prayer book recognizes that this won't necessarily be the case (see p. 480). Make the decision to include or exclude the celebration of Holy Communion in conversation with the officiating priest. The Greek word *Eucharist* means "Thanksgiving." When we gather at the Lord's Table, sharing the bread and wine and intentionally giving thanks to God for the person who has died and Christ's actions on our behalf, the Eucharist enhances the worship experience.

It may be that your family will decide not to include the Eucharist because your are concerned that non-Christian people who attend the service may feel excluded. This is a reasonable concern; however, most people attending a funeral expect that the traditions of the person who died will be observed. Rarely, if ever, will you hear that someone has taken offense by the offering of the Eucharist at an Episcopal funeral.

Ask that the guidelines for receiving Holy Communion be clearly articulated verbally and in writing in the bulletin. For those who prefer not to receive the bread and wine, the priest may offer a blessing instead.

The Committal

If remains are present at the church, it is customary to immediately follow the funeral with a committal service at a cemetery or columbarium. When the burial site is too far away from the church, the committal may take place at a later date.

Scattering of Ashes

It is permitted to scatter ashes in a memorial garden or other consecrated ground, but local ordinances must be observed, and they vary greatly from state to state. In any case, treat the cremated remains of the person who has died with the utmost respect and reverence.

Donating the Body to Science

It has become more and more common that organs or the entire body might be donated to science after someone has died. Most of us have had a chance to consider organ donation at different times of our life, and I strongly support it. If the person who has died has arranged to give their body for medical research, a standard protocol concerning the final resting place for the body should be addressed and a proper committal service should take place at the appropriate time.

The Importance of a Reception

While the funeral service in the church is paramount, it is also important to provide a reception or social gathering afterward. People often come long distances to pay their respects to the person who has died; give everyone a chance to share their own memories and to let the family know how much that person will be missed. I remember from the funeral for my own father that the church service was quite nice, but at the reception afterward I was overwhelmed by statements of appreciation and gratitude for my father. We all told stories and shared memories that heightened the significance of the gathering. It is often at the time after the funeral when we truly begin to understand the impact a life can have on others.

Many churches have parish halls and volunteer groups that can help to arrange for a reception. If members of the family or close friends live locally, it is also appropriate to host a gathering at their home. However, those who are most affected by a death should be careful to not take on too many responsibilities during a profound time of loss.

Seven Tips about what to Say and Do to Comfort Others

by Steven V. Malec

When comforting those who mourn, do not allow your own sense of helplessness to restrain you from reaching out to the bereaved. Recognize the therapeutic value of your presence. You can help a grieving person by:

1. Giving them your listening presence. Support is based more on effective listening than on any words you may say.

2. Giving them permission to grieve and express their feelings. Allow them to talk. Don't be afraid of their tears.

3. Remembering with them. Share stories, memories and photos. Use the deceased loved one's name.

4. Offering continued support. Visit, email, text, telephone and write them, especially around difficult days: birthdays, anniversaries, holidays or other special occasions.

5. Avoiding use of clichés. Speak from your heart.

6. Offering practical help. Cook a meal, take them to the store, library, cemetery, etc.

7. Praying with them. Offer to attend church with them. Give them a book of poems and prayers.

Many times, simple acts can facilitate much healing.

Scripture Readings

Introduction

The Starting Place

Begin the planning for a funeral or memorial service by selecting the scripture that will be read. The Book of Common Prayer (BCP) lists the scriptures to be used at the service. As a family, you will want to select scriptures that carry special meaning for you; decide on these with the help of your priest. Consider if any of these passages held special meaning for the one who has died. (Consult the form on p. 53, if filled in.)

The Episcopal Church has authorized the use of a number of Bible translations, including the *New Revised Standard Version of the Bible (NRSV)*, the *King James* or *Authorized Version* (the historic Bible of The Episcopal Church), the *New American Bible*, the *New International Version* and the *Revised Standard Version*. If you wish, check with your priest to identify additional Bible versions approved for use.

The passages below are from the *NRSV*, unless otherwise noted.

What Is Required

The instruction in the BCP reads, "One or more of the following passages from Holy Scripture is read. If there is to be a Communion, a passage from the Gospel always concludes the Readings" (pp. 470, 494). The minimal requirement is to have a single passage from scripture. There is no maximum number that can be used.

Three passages is usually a good number— read one passage from Hebrew Scripture (Old Testament) *or* one from the New Testament, then a psalm, then conclude with a gospel passage.

If a Eucharist is included in the service, a gospel passage is required.

A Note about the Psalms

Consider including a psalm as one of the scripture passages because they have powerful language about grief, loss and hope. If the psalm is prayed together, then all who have gathered can participate and lend their voices to expressions of trust in God even at a profound time of loss. The psalm can be prayed in unison or read responsively with the officiant or reader alternating verses with the congregation. (Some psalms lend themselves more easily to responsive reading, especially for participants unfamiliar with this form of community response.)

There are two translations of the psalms that are typically used in Episcopal services: The traditional Rite One version and the Rite Two contemporary language version—both versions are included below. The psalms were meant to be sung when they were first written, and there are many hymn settings of psalm texts if the family would prefer to sing the psalm.

Poetry or Other Non-Scripture Readings

Readings from other sources may be included in the service, however it is with the officiating minister's discretion. It is always best to seek guidance from the clergy before selecting readings that are not from scripture.

Hebrew Scripture

Isaiah 25:6-9

He will swallow up death forever.

On this mountain the Lord of hosts will make for all peoples a feast of rich food, a feast of well-aged wines, of rich food filled with marrow, of well-aged wines strained clear. And he will destroy on this mountain the shroud that is cast over all peoples, the sheet that is spread over all nations; he will swallow up death forever. Then the Lord God will wipe away the tears from all faces, and the disgrace of his people he will take away from all the earth, for the Lord has spoken. It will be said on that day, Lo, this is our God; we have waited for him, so that he might save us. This is the Lord for whom we have waited; let us be glad and rejoice in his salvation.

Isaiah 61:1-3

Comfort those who mourn.

The spirit of the Lord God is upon me, because the Lord has anointed me; he has sent me to bring good news to the oppressed, to bind up the brokenhearted, to proclaim liberty to the captives, and release to the prisoners; to proclaim the year of the Lord's favor, and the day of vengeance of our God; to comfort all who mourn; to provide for those who mourn in Zion—to give them a garland instead of ashes, the oil of gladness instead of mourning, the mantle of praise instead of a faint spirit. They will be called oaks of righteousness, the planting of the Lord, to display his glory.

Lamentations 3:22-26, 31-33

The Lord is good to those who wait for him.

The steadfast love of the Lord never ceases, his mercies never come to an end; they are new every morning; great is your faithfulness. "The Lord is my portion," says my soul, "therefore I will hope in him." The Lord is good to those who wait for him, to the soul that seeks him. It is good that one should wait quietly for the salvation of the Lord. For the Lord will not reject forever. Although he causes grief, he will have compassion according to the abundance of his steadfast love; for he does not willingly afflict or grieve anyone.

Wisdom 3:1-5, 9

The souls of the righteous are in the hand of God.

The souls of the righteous are in the hand of God, and no torment will ever touch them. In the eyes of the foolish they seemed to have died, and their departure was thought to be a disaster, and their going from us to be their destruction; but they are at peace. For though in the sight of others they were punished, their hope is full of immortality. Having been disciplined a little, they will receive great good, because God tested them and found them worthy of himself... Those who trust in him will understand truth, and the faithful will abide with him in love, because grace and mercy are upon his holy ones, and he watches over his elect.

Job 19:21-27a

I know that my Redeemer lives.

Job answered, "Have pity on me, have pity on me, O you my friends, for the hand of God has touched me! Why do you, like God, pursue me, never satisfied with my flesh? O that my words were written down! O that they were inscribed in a book! O that with an iron pen and with lead they were engraved on a rock forever! For I know that my Redeemer lives, and that at the last he will stand upon the earth; and after my skin has been thus destroyed, then in my flesh I shall see God, whom I shall see on my side, and my eyes shall behold, and not another."

Psalms

Psalm 23 (Dominus regit)

King James Version

The LORD is my shepherd; *
    I shall not want.
He maketh me to lie down in green pastures; *
    he leadeth me beside the still waters.
He restoreth my soul; *
    he leadeth me in the paths of righteous-
        ness for his Name's sake.
Yea, though I walk through the valley of the
        shadow of death,
I will fear no evil; *
    for thou art with me;
    thy rod and thy staff, they comfort me.
Thou preparest a table before me in the presence
        of mine enemies; *
    thou anointest my head with oil;
    my cup runneth over.
Surely goodness and mercy shall follow me all
        the days of my life, *
    and I will dwell in the house of the LORD
        for ever.

Psalm 23 (Dominus regit me)

(as found in The Psalter)

The LORD is my shepherd; *
    I shall not be in want.
He makes me lie down in green pastures *
    and leads me beside still waters.
He revives my soul *
    and guides me along right pathways for his
        Name's sake.
Though I walk through the valley of the shadow
    of death,

I shall fear no evil; *
    for you are with me;
    your rod and your staff, they comfort me.
You spread a table before me in the presence of
        those who trouble me; *
    you have anointed my head with oil,
    and my cup is running over.
Surely your goodness and mercy shall follow me
        all the days of my life, *
    and I will dwell in the house of the LORD
        for ever.

Psalm 23 (Dominus regit me)

(as found in The Burial of the Dead, Rite One)

The LORD is my shepherd; *
    therefore can I lack nothing.
He shall feed me in a green pasture, *
    and lead me forth beside the waters of
        comfort.
He shall convert my soul, *
    and bring me forth in the paths of righ-
        teousness for his Name's sake.
Yea, though I walk through the valley of the
        shadow of death,
I will fear no evil; *
    for thou art with me;
    thy rod and thy staff comfort me.
Thou shalt prepare a table before me in the
        presence of them that trouble me; *
    thou hast anointed my head with oil,
    and my cup shall be full.
Surely thy loving-kindness and mercy shall
        follow me all the days of my life; *
    and I will dwell in the house of the LORD
        for ever.

Psalm 27 1,5-12, 17-18 (Dominus illuminatio)
(as found in The Psalter)

The LORD is my light and my salvation;
whom then shall I fear? *
   the LORD is the strength of my life;
   of whom then shall I be afraid?
One thing have I asked of the LORD;
one thing I seek; *
   that I may dwell in the house of the LORD all
      the days of my life;
To behold the fair beauty of the LORD *
   and to seek him in his temple.
For in the day of trouble he shall keep me safe
      in his shelter; *
   he shall hide me in the secrecy of his
      dwelling
   and set me high upon a rock.
Even now he lifts up my head *
   above my enemies round about me.
Therefore I will offer in his dwelling an oblation
with sounds of great gladness; *
   I will sing and make music to the LORD.
Hearken to my voice, O LORD, when I call; *
   have mercy on me and answer me.
You speak in my heart and say, "Seek my face." *
   Your face, LORD, will I seek.
Hide not your face from me, *
   nor turn away your servant in displeasure.
What if I had not believed
that I should see the goodness of the LORD *
   in the land of the living!
O tarry and await the LORD's pleasure;
be strong, and he shall comfort your heart; *
   wait patiently for the LORD.

Psalm 27 (Dominus illuminatio)
(as found in The Burial of the Dead, Rite One)

The LORD is my light and my salvation;
whom then shall I fear? *
   the LORD is the strength of my life;
   of whom then shall I be afraid?
One thing have I desired of the LORD, which
      I will require, *
   even that I may dwell in the house of the
      LORD all the days of my life,
   to behold the fair beauty of the LORD, and to
      visit his temple.
For in the time of trouble he shall hide me in
      his tabernacle; *
   yea, in the secret place of his dwelling shall
      he hide me,
   and set me up upon a rock of stone.
And now shall he lift up mine head *
   above mine enemies round about me.
Therefore will I offer in his dwelling an oblation
      with great gladness; *
   I will sing and speak praises unto the LORD.
Hearken unto my voice, O LORD, when I cry
      unto thee; *
   have mercy upon me, and hear me.
My heart hath talked of thee, Seek ye my face. *
   Thy face, LORD, will I seek.
O hide not thou thy face from me, *
   nor cast thy servant away in displeasure.
I should utterly have fainted, *
   but that I believe verily to see the goodness
      of the LORD in the land of the living.
O tarry thou the LORD's leisure; *
   be strong, and he shall comfort thine heart;
   and put thou thy trust in the LORD.

Psalm 42:1-7 (Quemadmodum)

(as found in The Psalter)

As the deer longs for the water-brooks, *
  so longs my soul for you, O God.
My soul is athirst for God, athirst for the living
    God; *
  when shall I come to appear before the
    presence of God?
My tears have been my food day and night, *
  while all day long they say to me,
  "Where now is your God?"
I pour out my soul when I think on these things: *
  how I went with the multitude and led them
    into the house of God,
With the voice of praise and thanksgiving, *
  among those who keep holy-day.
Why are you so full of heaviness, O my soul? *
  and why are you so disquieted within me?
Put your trust in God; *
  for I will yet give thanks to him,
  who is the help of my countenance, and my
    God.

Psalm 42 (Quemadmodum)

(as found in The Burial of the Dead, Rite One)

Like as the hart desireth the water-brooks, *
  so longeth my soul after thee, O God.
My soul is athirst for God, yea, even for the
    living God; *
  when shall I come to appear before the pres-
    ence of God?
My tears have been my meat day and night, *
  while they daily say unto me, Where is now
    thy God?
Now when I think thereupon, I pour out my
    heart by myself; *
  for I went with the multitude, and brought
    them forth into the house of God;
In the voice of praise and thanksgiving, *

among such as keep holy-day.
Why art thou so full of heaviness, O my soul? *
  and why art thou so disquieted within me ?
O put thy trust in God; *
  for I will yet thank him, which is the help of
    my countenance, and my God.

Psalm 46:1-3, 5,6,11,12 (Deus noster refugium)

(as found in The Psalter)

God is our refuge and strength, *
  a very present help in trouble.
Therefore we will not fear, though the earth be
    moved, *
  and though the mountains be toppled into
    the depths of the sea;
Though its waters rage and foam, *
  and though the mountains tremble at its
    tumult.
There is a river whose streams make glad the city
    of God, *
  the holy habitation of the Most High.
God is in the midst of her;
she shall not be overthrown; *
  God shall help her at the break of day.
Be still, then, and know that I am God; *
  I will be exalted among the nations;
  I will be exalted in the earth.
The LORD of hosts is with us; *
  the God of Jacob is our stronghold.

Psalm 46:1-3, 5,6,11,12 (Deus noster refugium)

(as found in The Burial of the Dead, Rite One)

God is our hope and strength, *
  a very present help in trouble.
Therefore will we not fear, though the earth be
    moved,; *
  and though the hills be carried into the midst
    of the sea;
Though the waters thereof rage and swell, *

and though the mountains shake at the
tempest of the same.
There is a river, the streams whereof make glad
the city of God, *
the holy place of the tabernacle of the Most
Highest.
God is in the midst of her,
therefore shall she not be removed; *
God shall help her, and that right early.
Be still then, and know that I am God; *
I will be exalted among the nations,
and I will be exalted in the earth.
The LORD of hosts is with us; *
the God of Jacob is our refuge.

Psalm 90:1-10,12 (Domine, refugium)

(as found in The Psalter)

LORD, you have been our refuge *
from one generation to another.
Before the mountains were brought forth,
or the land and the earth were born, *
from age to age you are God.
You turn us back to the dust and say, *
"Go back, O child of earth."
For a thousand years in your sight are like
yesterday when it is past *
and like a watch in the night.
You sweep us away like a dream; *
we fade away suddenly like the grass.
In the morning it is green and flourishes; *
in the evening it is dried up and withered.
For we consume away in your displeasure; *
we are afraid because of your wrathful
indignation.
Our iniquities you have set before you, *
and our secret sins in the light of your
countenance.
When you are angry, all our days are gone; *
we bring our years to an end like a sigh.
The span of our life is seventy years,

perhaps in strength even eighty; *
yet the sum of them is but labor and sorrow,
for they pass away quickly and we are gone.
So teach us to number our days *
that we may apply our hearts to wisdom.

Psalm 90:1-10,12 (Domine, refugium)

(as found in The Burial of the Dead, Rite One)

LORD, thou hast been our refuge, *
from one generation to another.
Before the mountains were brought forth,
or ever the earth and the world were made, *
thou art God from everlasting, and world
without end.
Thou turnest man to destruction; *
again thou sayest, Come again, ye children of
men.
For a thousand years in thy sight are but as
yesterday when it is past, *
and as a watch in the night.
As soon as thou scatterest them they are even as
a sleep, *
and fade away suddenly like the grass.
In the morning it is green, and groweth up; *
but in the evening it is cut down, dried up,
and withered.
For we consume away in thy displeasure, *
and are afraid at thy wrathful indignation.
Thou hast set our misdeeds before thee, *
and our secret sins in the light of thy
countenance.
For when thou art angry all our days are gone; *
we bring our years to an end, as it were a tale
that is told.
The days of our age are threescore years and ten;
and though men be so strong that they come to
fourscore years, *
yet is their strength then but labor and
sorrow,
so soon passeth it away, and we are gone.

So teach us to number our days, *
    that we may apply our hearts unto wisdom.

Psalm 106:1-5 (Confitemini Domino)
(as found in The Psalter)

Hallelujah!
Give thanks to the LORD, for he is good, *
    for his mercy endures for ever.
Who can declare the mighty acts of the LORD *
    or show forth all his praise?
Happy are those who act with justice *
    and always do what is right!
Remember me, O LORD, with the favor you have
      for your people, *
    and visit me with your saving help;
That I may see the prosperity of your elect
and be glad with the gladness of your people, *
    that I may glory with your inheritance.

Psalm 106:1-5 (Confitemini Domino)
(as found in The Burial of the Dead, Rite One)

O give thanks unto the LORD, for he is gracious, *
    and his mercy endureth for ever.
Who can express the noble acts of the LORD, *
    or show forth all his praise?
Blessed are they that alway keep judgment, *
    and do righteousness.
Remember me, O LORD, according to the favor
      that thou bearest unto thy people; *
    O visit me with thy salvation;
That I may see the felicity of thy chosen, *
    and rejoice in the gladness of thy people,
    and give thanks with thine inheritance.

Psalm 116:1-8, 12-13 (Dilexi, quoniam)
(as found in The Psalter)

I love the LORD, because he has heard the voice
    of my supplication, *
because he has inclined his ear to me
    whenever I called upon him.

The cords of death entangled me;
the grip of the grave took hold of me; *
    I came to grief and sorrow.
Then I called upon the Name of the LORD: *
    "O LORD, I pray you, save my life."
Gracious is the LORD and righteous; *
    our God is full of compassion.
The LORD watches over the innocent; *
    I was brought very low, and he helped me.
Turn again to your rest, O my soul, *
    for the LORD has treated you well.
For you have rescued my life from death, *
    my eyes from tears, and my feet from
      stumbling.
I will walk in the presence of the LORD *
    in the land of the living.
I will fulfill my vows to the LORD *
    in the presence of all his people.
Precious in the sight of the LORD *
    is the death of his servants.

Psalm 116:1-8, 12-13 (Dilexi, quoniam)
(as found in The Burial of the Dead, Rite One)

My delight is in the LORD, *
    because he hath heard the voice of my prayer;
Because he hath inclined his ear unto me, *
    therefore will I call upon him as long as I
      live.
The snares of death compassed me round about, *
    and the pains of hell gat hold upon me.
I found trouble and heaviness;
then called I upon the Name of the LORD; *
    O LORD, I beseech thee, deliver my soul.
Gracious is the LORD, and righteous; *
    yea, our God is merciful.
The LORD preserveth the simple; *
    I was in misery, and he helped me.
Turn again then unto thy rest, O my soul, *
    for the LORD hath rewarded thee.
Any why? thou hast delivered my soul from
      death, *

mine eyes from tears, and my feet from
   falling.
I will walk before the LORD *
   in the land of the living.
I will pay my vows now in the presence of all his
   people; *
   right dear in the sight of the LORD is the
   death of his saints.

Psalm 121 *(Levavi oculos)*
(as found in The Psalter)

I lift up my eyes to the hills; *
   from where is my help to come?
My help comes from the LORD, *
   the maker of heaven and earth.
He will not let your foot be moved *
   and he who watches over you will not fall
   asleep.
Behold, he who keeps watch over Israel *
   shall neither slumber nor sleep;
The LORD himself watches over you; *
   the LORD is your shade at your right hand,
So that the sun shall not strike you by day, *
   nor the moon by night.
The LORD shall preserve you from all evil; *
   it is he who shall keep you safe.
The LORD shall watch over your going out and
   your coming in, *
   from this time forth for evermore.

Psalm 121 *(Levavi oculos)*
(as found in The Burial of the Dead, Rite One)

I will lift up mine eyes unto the hills; *
   from whence cometh my help?
My help cometh even from the LORD, *
   who hath made heaven and earth.
He will not suffer thy foot to be moved, *
   and he that keepeth thee will not sleep.
Behold, he that keepeth Israel *
   shall neither slumber nor sleep.

The LORD himself is thy keeper; *
   the LORD is thy defence upon thy right hand;
So that the sun shall not burn thee by day, *
   neither the moon by night.
The LORD shall preserve thee from all evil; *
   yea, it is even he that shall keep thy soul.
The LORD shall preserve thy going out, and thy
   coming in, *
   from this time forth for evermore.

Psalm 130 *(De profundis)*
(as found in The Psalter)

Out of the depths have I called to you, O LORD;
LORD, hear my voice; *
   let your ears consider well the voice of my
   supplication.
If you, LORD, were to note what is done amiss, *
   O LORD, who could stand?
For there is forgiveness with you; *
   therefore you shall be feared.
I wait for the LORD; my soul waits for him; *
   in his word is my hope.
My soul waits for the LORD,
more than watchmen for the morning, *
   more than watchmen for the morning.
O Israel, wait for the LORD, *
   for with the LORD there is mercy;
With him there is plenteous redemption, *
   and he shall redeem Israel
      from all their sins.

Psalm 130 *(De profundis)*
(as found in The Burial of the Dead, Rite One)

Out of the deep have I called unto thee, O LORD; *
   LORD, hear my voice.
O let thine ears consider well *
   the voice of my complaint.
If thou, LORD, wilt be extreme to mark what is
   done amiss, *
   O LORD, who may abide it?

For there is mercy with thee, *
>   therefore shalt thou be feared.
I look for the Lord; my soul doth wait for him; *
>   in his word is my trust.
My soul fleeth unto the Lord before the morn-
>   ing watch; *
>   I say, before the morning watch.
O Israel, trust in the Lord,
for with the Lord there is mercy, *
>   and with him is plenteous redemption.
And he shall redeem Israel *
>   from all his sins.

Psalm 139 (Domine, probasti)

(as found in The Psalter)

Lord, you have searched me out and known me; *
>   you know my sitting down and my rising up;
>   you discern my thoughts from afar.
You trace my journeys and my resting-places *
>   and are acquainted with all my ways.
Indeed, there is not a word on my lips, *
>   but you, O Lord, know it altogether.
You press upon me behind and before *
>   and lay your hand upon me.
Such knowledge is too wonderful for me; *
>   it is so high that I cannot attain to it.
Where can I go then from your Spirit? *
>   where can I flee from your presence?
If I climb up to heaven, you are there; *
>   if I make the grave my bed, you are there
>   also.
If I take the wings of the morning *
>   and dwell in the uttermost parts of the sea,
Even there your hand will lead me *
>   and your right hand hold me fast.
If I say, "Surely the darkness will cover me, *
>   and the light around me turn to night,"
Darkness is not dark to you;
the night is as bright as the day; *
>   darkness and light to you are both alike.

Psalm 139 (Domine, probasti)

(as found in The Burial of the Dead, Rite One)

O Lord, thou hast searched me out, and known
>   me. *
>   Thou knowest my down-sitting and mine
>   up-rising;
>   thou understandest my thoughts long before.
Thou art about my path, and about my bed, *
>   and art acquainted with all my ways.
For lo, there is not a word in my tongue, *
>   but thou, O Lord, knowest it altogether.
Thou hast beset me behind and before, *
>   and laid thine hand upon me.
Such knowledge is too wonderful and excellent
>   for me; *
>   I cannot attain unto it.
Whither shall I go then from thy Spirit? *
>   or whither shall I go then from thy presence?
If I climb up into heaven, thou art there; *
>   if I go down to hell, thou art there also.
If I take the wings of the morning, *
>   and remain in the uttermost parts of the sea;
Even there also shall thy hand lead me, *
>   and thy right hand shall hold me.
If I say, Peradventure the darkness shall cover me, *
>   then shall my night be turned to day.
Yea, the darkness is no darkness with thee,
but the night is as clear as day; *
>   the darkness and light to thee are both alike.

New Testament

Romans 8:14-19, 34-35, 37-39
The glory that shall be revealed.

All who are led by the Spirit of God are children of God. For you did not receive a spirit of slavery to fall back into fear, but you have received a spirit of adoption. When we cry, "Abba! Father!" it is that very Spirit bearing witness with our spirit that we are children of God, and if children, then heirs, heirs of God and joint heirs with Christ—if, in fact, we suffer with him so that we may also be glorified with him.

I consider that the sufferings of this present time are not worth comparing with the glory about to be revealed to us. For the creation waits with eager longing for the revealing of the children of God...

Who is to condemn? It is Christ Jesus, who died, yes, who was raised, who is at the right hand of God, who indeed intercedes for us. Who will separate us from the love of Christ? Will hardship, or distress, or persecution, or famine, or nakedness, or peril, or sword? No, in all these things we are more than conquerors through him who loved us. For I am convinced that neither death, nor life, nor angels, nor rulers, nor things present, nor things to come, nor powers, nor height, nor depth, nor anything else in all creation, will be able to separate us from the love of God in Christ Jesus our Lord.

1 Corinthians 15:20-26, 35-38, 42-44, 53-58
The imperishable body.

But in fact Christ has been raised from the dead, the first fruits of those who have died. For since death came through a human being, the resurrection of the dead has also come through a human being; for as all die in Adam, so all will be made alive in Christ. But each in his own order: Christ the first fruits, then at his coming those who belong to Christ. Then comes the end, when he hands over the kingdom to God the Father, after he has destroyed every ruler and every authority and power. For he must reign until he has put all his enemies under his feet. The last enemy to be destroyed is death.

But someone will ask, "How are the dead raised? With what kind of body do they come?" Fool! What you sow does not come to life unless it dies. And as for what you sow, you do not sow the body that is to be, but a bare seed, perhaps of wheat or of some other grain. But God gives it a body as he has chosen, and to each kind of seed its own body.

So it is with the resurrection of the dead. What is sown is perishable, what is raised is imperishable. It is sown in dishonor, it is raised in glory. It is sown in weakness, it is raised in power. It is sown a physical body, it is raised a spiritual body. If there is a physical body, there is also a spiritual body.

For this perishable body must put on imperishability, and this mortal body must put on immortality. When this perishable body puts on imperishability, and this mortal body puts on immortality, then the saying that is written will be fulfilled:

> "Death has been swallowed up in victory."
> "Where, O death, is your victory?
> Where, O death, is your sting?"

The sting of death is sin, and the power of sin is the law. But thanks be to God, who gives us the victory through our Lord Jesus Christ.

Therefore, my beloved, be steadfast, immovable, always excelling in the work of the Lord, because you know that in the Lord your labor is not in vain.

2 Corinthians 4:16-5:9
Things that are unseen are eternal.

So we do not lose heart. Even though our outer nature is wasting away, our inner nature is being renewed day by day. For this slight momentary affliction is preparing us for an eternal weight of glory beyond all measure, because we look not at what can be seen but at what cannot be seen; for what can be seen is temporary, but what cannot be seen is eternal.

For we know that if the earthly tent we live in is destroyed, we have a building from God, a house not made with hands, eternal in the heavens. For in this tent we groan, longing to be clothed with our heavenly dwelling—if indeed, when we have taken it off we will not be found naked. For while we are still in this tent, we groan under our burden, because we wish not to be unclothed but to be further clothed, so that what is mortal may be swallowed up by life. He who has prepared us

for this very thing is God, who has given us the Spirit as a guarantee.

So we are always confident; even though we know that while we are at home in the body we are away from the Lord—for we walk by faith, not by sight. Yes, we do have confidence, and we would rather be away from the body and at home with the Lord. So whether we are at home or away, we make it our aim to please him.

1 John 3:1-2
We shall be like him.

See what love the Father has given us, that we should be called children of God; and that is what we are. The reason the world does not know us is that it did not know him. Beloved, we are God's children now; what we will be has not yet been revealed. What we do know is this: when he is revealed, we will be like him, for we will see him as he is.

Revelation 7:9-17
God will wipe away every tear.

After this I looked, and there was a great multitude that no one could count, from every nation, from all tribes and peoples and languages, standing before the throne and before the Lamb, robed in white, with palm branches in their hands. They cried out in a loud voice, saying,

> "Salvation belongs to our God who is seated
> on the throne, and to the Lamb!"

And all the angels stood around the throne and around the elders and the four living creatures, and they fell on their faces before the throne and worshiped God, singing,

> "Amen! Blessing and glory and wisdom
> and thanksgiving and honor
> and power and might
> be to our God forever and ever! Amen."

Then one of the elders addressed me, saying, "Who are these, robed in white, and where have they come from?" I said to him, "Sir, you are the one that knows." Then he said to me, "These are they who have come out of the great ordeal; they have washed their robes and made them white in the blood of the Lamb.

> For this reason they are before the throne
> of God,
> > and worship him day and night within
> > his temple,
> > and the one who is seated on the throne
> > will shelter them.
> They will hunger no more, and thirst
> no more;
> > the sun will not strike them,
> > nor any scorching heat;
> for the Lamb at the center of the throne will
> be their shepherd,
> > and he will guide them to springs of the
> > water of life,
> > and God will wipe away every tear from
> > their eyes."

Revelation 21:2-7
Behold, I make all things new.

And I saw the holy city, the new Jerusalem, coming down out of heaven from God, prepared as a bride adorned for her husband. And I heard a loud voice from the throne saying,

> "See, the home of God is among mortals.
> He will dwell with them as their God;
> they will be his peoples,
> and God himself will be with them;
> he will wipe every tear from their eyes.
> Death will be no more;
> mourning and crying and pain will be
> > no more,
> for the first things have passed away."

And the one who was seated on the throne said, "See, I am making all things new." Also he said, "Write this, for these words are trustworthy and true." Then he said to me, "It is done! I am the Alpha and the Omega, the beginning and the end. To the thirsty I will give water as a gift from the spring of the water of life. Those who conquer will inherit these things, and I will be their God and they will be my children."

Gospel Readings

John 5:24-27

He who believes has everlasting life.

Jesus said, "Very truly, I tell you, anyone who hears my word and believes him who sent me has eternal life, and does not come under judgment, but has passed from death to life.

"Very truly, I tell you, the hour is coming, and is now here, when the dead will hear the voice of the Son of God, and those who hear will live. For just as the Father has life in himself, so he has granted the Son also to have life in himself; and he has given him authority to execute judgment, because he is the Son of Man."

John 6:37-40

All that the Father gives me will come to me.

Jesus said, "Everything that the Father gives me will come to me, and anyone who comes to me I will never drive away; for I have come down from heaven, not to do my own will, but the will of him who sent me. And this is the will of him who sent me, that I should lose nothing of all that he has given me, but raise it up on the last day. This is indeed the will of my Father, that all who see the Son and believe in him may have eternal life; and I will raise them up on the last day."

John 10:11-16

I am the good shepherd.

Jesus said, "I am the good shepherd. The good shepherd lays down his life for the sheep. The hired hand, who is not the shepherd and does not own the sheep, sees the wolf coming and leaves the sheep and runs away—and the wolf snatches them and scatters them. The hired hand runs away because a hired hand does not care for the sheep. I am the good shepherd. I know my own and my own know me, just as the Father knows me and I know the Father. And I lay down my life for the sheep. I have other sheep that do not belong to this fold. I must bring them also, and they will listen to my voice. So there will be one flock, one shepherd."

John 11:21-27

I am the resurrection and the life.

Martha said to Jesus, "Lord, if you had been here, my brother would not have died. But even now I know that God will give you whatever you ask of him." Jesus said to her, "Your brother will rise again." Martha said to him, "I know that he will rise again in the resurrection on the last day." Jesus said to her, "I am the resurrection and the life. Those who believe in me, even though they die, will live, and everyone who lives and believes in me will never die. Do you believe this?" She said to him, "Yes, Lord, I believe that you are the Messiah, the Son of God, the one coming into the world."

John 14:1-6

In my Father's house are many rooms.

Jesus said to his disciples, "Do not let your hearts be troubled. Believe in God, believe also in me. In my Father's house there are many dwelling places. If it were not so, would I have told you that I go to prepare a place for you? And if I go and prepare a place for you, I will come again and will take you to myself, so that where I am, there you may be also. And you know the way to the place where I am going." Thomas said to him, "Lord, we do not know where you are going. How can we know the way?" Jesus said to him, "I am the way, and the truth, and the life. No one comes to the Father except through me."

Music Suggestions

Introduction

The Starting Place

The Episcopal Church incorporates a diversity of musical styles. Typically the priest, in conjunction with the organist or music director, develops guidelines for using music in worship; you may want to request a copy of these. Those planning the liturgy will do their best to make sure that the music selected supports the scripture readings that have been chosen.

Share your ideas and requests with your priest, including those that may have been identified in advance using the form found on page 53.

One Church, Many Hymnals

The Episcopal Church has several music collections and hymnals that have been approved for use by the church. The three most common hymnals found in churches today are:

The Hymnal 1982 (traditional hymns)

Lift Every Voice and Sing II (an African-American hymnal)

Wonder, Love, and Praise (a supplement to *The Hymnal 1982* that includes a variety of musical styles including contemporary hymns, chants and new texts set to familiar tunes)

Hymns

Opening Hymn/Processional Hymn

The Hymnal 1982

8	Morning has broken
178	Alleluia, alleluia! Give thanks to the risen Lord
194/195	Jesus lives! thy terrors now
199/200	Come ye faithful raise the strain
208	Alleluia! The strife is o'er, the battle done
287	For all the saints
293	I sing a song of the saints of God
362	Holy, holy, holy
376	Joyful, joyful we adore thee
405	All things bright and beautiful
410	Praise my soul, the King of heaven
423	Immortal, invisible, God only wise
455/456	O love of God, how strong and true
482	Lord of all hopefulness
488	Be thou my vision
535	Ye servants of God
558	Faith of our fathers
608	Eternal Father, strong to save
618	Ye watchers and ye holy ones
620	Jerusalem, my happy home
637	How firm a foundation
653	Dear Lord and Father of mankind
657	Love divine, all loves excelling
671	Amazing Grace
680	O God our help in ages past
686	Come thou fount of every blessing
687/688	A mighty fortress is our God
690	Guide me, O thou great Jehovah

Lift Every Voice and Sing II

60	How great thou art
101	Softly and tenderly Jesus is calling
106	Precious Lord, take my hand
183	God will take care of you
184	Blessed assurance
188	It is well with my soul
189	Great is thy faithfulness
218	Jesus loves me! this I know

Wonder, Love, and Praise

775	Give thanks for life

Hymn Settings of Psalms

The Hymnal 1982

517	Psalm 84 How lovely is your dwelling place
645/646	Psalm 23 The King of love my shepherd is
664	Psalm 23 My shepherd will supply my need
658	Psalm 42 As longs the deer for cooling streams
680	Psalm 90 O God our help in ages past
687/688	Psalm 46 A mighty fortress is our God

Wonder, Love, and Praise

764	Psalm 34 Taste and See
810	Psalm 91 On Eagles' wings

Between Readings or at Communion

The Hymnal 1982

304	I come with joy to meet my Lord
316	This is the hour of banquet and of song
335	I am the bread of life
339	Deck thyself, my soul, with gladness
354	Into paradise may the angels lead you

355	Give rest, O Christ, to thy servant
356	May choirs of angels lead you
357	Jesus, Son of Mary
358	Christ the Victorious, give to your servants
416	For the beauty of the earth
433	We gather together
455	O love of God, how strong and true
469/470	There's a wideness in God's mercy
482	Lord of all hopefulness
487	Come, my way, my truth, my life
488	Be thou my vision
508	Breathe on me breath of God
510	Come Holy Spirit, heavenly dove
517	How lovely is your dwelling place
593	Lord make us servants of your peace
645/646	The King of love my shepherd is
660	O Master, let me walk with thee
662	Abide with me
676	There is a balm in Gilead

Lift Every Voice and Sing II

8	Deep River
16	Yahweh, I know you are near
19	Wayfaring stranger
69	In the garden
111	Come thou fount of every blessing
152	Let us break bread together
154	Taste and See
188	When peace like a river/It is well with my soul
194	Lead me, guide me
203	There is a balm in Gilead

Wonder, Love, and Praise

764	Taste and See
810	On Eagles' wings
811	You shall cross the barren dessert
825	Bless the Lord my soul

Final Hymn/Recessional

The Hymnal 1982

7	Christ, whose glory fills the skies
180	He is risen, he is risen
194/195	Jesus lives! thy terrors now
207	Jesus Christ is risen today
208	Alleluia! The strife is o'er, the battle done
287	For all the saints
335	I am the bread of life
376	Joyful, joyful we adore thee
397	Now thanks we all our God
400	All creatures of our God and King
405	All things bright and beautiful
562	Onward Christian soldiers
599	Lift every voice and sing
608	Eternal Father strong to save
620	Jerusalem, my happy home
625	Ye holy angels bright
657	Love divine, all loves excelling
665	All my hope on God is founded
671	Amazing grace
680	O God our help in ages past
687/688	A mighty fortress is our God
690	Guide me, O thus great Jehovah

Lift Every Voice and Sing II

1	Lift every voice and sing
60	How great thou art
106	Precious Lord, take my hand
130	Glory, glory, hallelujah
183	God will take care of you
188	When peace like a river/It is well with my soul
189	Great is thy faithfulness
226	Mine eyes have seen the glory

Wonder, Love, and Praise

| 775 | Give thanks for life |

Vital Information for Survivors or Personal Representative

Name _____
    Last   First   Middle (or Initial)

Address _____
    Street   City   State   Zip

Telephone _____ Email _____ Social Security # _____ _____ _____

Date of Birth _____ Place of Birth _____
                                                                    City

Citizen of _____
                        Country

Resided in County for (how long) _____ in State (how long) _____

Single ____ Married ____ Partnered ____ Widowed ____ Divorced ____ Separated___

Name of Spouse/Partner _____ Alive _____ Deceased _____

Wedding Date/Anniversary _____ Occupation and Title (or retired from) _____

Type of Business/Employer _____ How Long_____

Father _____
        Name   Date of Birth   Birthplace

Mother _____
        Maiden Name   Date of Birth   Birthplace

Persons to Notify: Next of Kin Other than Spouse

Name	Address	Phone	Relationship
Email	Facebook	LinkedIn	Other
Name	Address	Phone	Relationship
Email	Facebook	LinkedIn	Other
Name	Address	Phone	Relationship
Email	Facebook	LinkedIn	Other
Name	Address	Phone	Relationship
Email	Facebook	LinkedIn	Other

Name	Address	Phone	Relationship
Email	Facebook	LinkedIn	Other
Name	Address	Phone	Relationship
Email	Facebook	LinkedIn	Other

Other Persons/Organizations

Church _____ Phone _____

  Email _____ Website _____

Doctor _____ Phone _____

  Email _____ Website _____

Funeral Home _____ Phone _____

  Email _____ Website _____

Personal Representative/Attorney _____ Phone _____

  Email _____ Website _____

Organizations

Name	Address	Phone	Relationship
Email	Facebook	Website	Other
Name	Address	Phone	Relationship
Email	Facebook	Website	Other
Name	Address	Phone	Relationship
Email	Facebook	Website	Other
Name	Address	Phone	Relationship
Email	Facebook	Website	Other

Financial Papers & Records

Where Records Located _____ Social Security Number _____

Will

I have a will. Yes _____ No _____ Will Dated _____ Where Located _____

Executor _____ Phone _____

    Email _____ Other _____

Attorney _____ Phone _____

    Email _____ Other _____

Additional Information _____

Banking

    Bank _____ Phone _____

    Address _____

    Website _____ Login/User Name _____ Password _____

    Type of Account(s) Checking # _____ Savings # _____ Other _____

    Bank _____ Phone _____

    Address _____

    Website _____ Login/User Name _____ Password _____

    Type of Account(s) Checking # _____ Savings # _____ Other _____

Safety Deposit Box _____

Number	Key Location	Bank
Address		Phone

Insurance Policies _____

Name	Policy Number	Company/Union/Organization/Agent	
Phone	Website	User Name	Password
Email			
Name	Policy Number	Company/Union/Organization/Agent	
Phone	Website	User Name	Password
Email			

Pension/Investments

Pension _____
       Name/Number   Administrator   Address

_____
       Website   User Name   Password

401/K Plan _____
       Name/Number   Administrator   Address

_____
       Website   User Name   Password

Investments _____
       Name/Number   Administrator   Address

_____
       Website   User Name   Password

_____
       Name/Number   Administrator   Address

_____
       Website   User Name   Password

Other Benefits

_____
       Name/Number   Administrator   Address

_____
       Website   User Name   Password

_____
       Name/Number   Administrator   Address

_____
       Website   User Name   Password

Veteran Information

Service Identification/Serial Number _____ Rank & Branch of Service_____

Location of Veteran's Office to Notify _____
       Address   Phone

Entered Service _____ Separated from Service _____
       Date/Place   Date/Place

Wars Fought _____ Medals or Honors _____

I would want American flag for my family _____ and military honors (if available) _____

Any other instructions or information (especially any things you don't want to take place).

_____

_____

Vital Information for the Funeral Home

Name _____
      Last   First   Middle (or Initial)

Address _____
      Street   City   State   Zip

Telephone _____ Email _____ Social Security # _____ _____ _____

Date of Birth _____ Place of Birth _____
                                           City

Citizen of _____
                 Country

Resided in County for (how long) _____ in State (how long) _____

Single ____ Married ____ Partnered ____ Widowed ____ Divorced ____ Separated ____

Name of Spouse/Partner _____ Alive _____ Deceased _____

Wedding Date/Anniversary _____ Occupation and Title (or retired from)

Type of Business/Employer _____ How Long _____

Father _____
      Name   Date of Birth   Birthplace

Mother _____
      Maiden Name   Date of Birth   Birthplace

Veteran Information

Service Identification/Serial Number _____ Rank & Branch of Service _____

Location of Veteran's Office to Notify _____
                                 Address   Phone

Website _____ User Name _____ Password _____

Entered Service _____ Separated from Service _____
           Date/Place   Date/Place

Wars Fought _____ Medals or Honors _____

I would want an American flag for my family _____ and military honors (if available) _____

Floral Request _____ _____

Gifts: Instead of flowers, I would prefer that my friends make memorial gifts to

Name	Address	Website
Name	Address	Website
Name	Address	Website

Final Disposition of My Body   ( ) Burial   ( ) Cremation ( ) Donation for Research

at: _____cemetery

I have ( ) or have not ( ) consulted with the above named cemetery regarding: a cemetery plot ( )

a vault ( )   crypt ( )   niche for created remains ( )   memorial marker ( ) services and a casket ( )

The location or number of my burial plot (cemetery, mausoleum, columbarium niche) or other instructions is

_____

I do wish ( )   I do not wish ( )   or ( ) let my family decide to have an open casket at calling hours.

If open: Clothing _____ Jewelry _____ Glasses on ( ) off ( )

Funeral Services

Type of Services

___ Rite One   ___ Remains Present in Church

___ Rite Two   ___ Burial Service

___ With Eucharist

___ Without Eucharist

I want to have these services conducted at ( ) Church _____

( ) Funeral Home _____   ( ) Other _____
            Date and time   Date and time

Clergy/Presider   1st Choice _____   2nd Choice _____

Eulogist   1st Choice _____   2nd Choice _____

Pallbearers   Name _____   Phone _____ Email _____

                  Name _____   Phone _____ Email _____

                  Name _____   Phone _____ Email _____

                  Name _____   Phone _____ Email _____

Other specific instructions not covered above _____

Funeral/Memorial Service Details

Scripture Readings   1st Reading _____   Reader _____ _____

                         2nd Reading _____   Reader _____

                         The Gospel _____   Priest _____

Music   _____   _____

             _____   _____

Other specific directions not covered above: _____ _____

_____

Signature _____   _____
                  Signature   Date

Witnesses _____ _____ _____ _____
             Signature   Date   Signature   Date

Reception

Location _____

Other Instructions _____

_____

_____

_____

This page may be torn out, copied and put in with your will and important papers or given to your church or personal representative.

Vital Information for the Parish Church

Name _____
      Last   First   Middle (or Initial)

Address _____
      Street   City   State   Zip

Telephone _____ Email _____ Social Security # _____ _____ _____

Date of Birth _____ Place of Birth _____
                                City

Citizen of _____
               Country

Resided in County for (how long) _____ in State (how long) _____

Single ____ Married ____ Partnered ____ Widowed ____ Divorced ____ Separated ____

Name of Spouse/Partner _____ Alive _____ Deceased _____

Wedding Date/Anniversary _____ Occupation and Title (or retired from)

Type of Business/Employer _____ How Long _____

Father _____ _____ _____
      Name   Date of Birth   Birthplace

Mother _____ _____ _____
      Maiden Name   Date of Birth   Birthplace

Veteran Information

Service Identification/Serial Number _____ Rank & Branch of Service _____

Location of Veteran's Office to Notify _____
                      Address   Phone

Website _____

Entered Service _____ Separated from Service _____
      Date/Place   Date/Place

Wars Fought _____ Medals or Honors _____

Floral Request _____ _____

Gifts: Instead of flowers, I would prefer that my friends make memorial gifts to

Name	Address	Website
Name	Address	Website
Name	Address	Website

Vital Information for the Parish Church (cont.)

Final Disposition of My Body   ( ) Burial   ( ) Cremation   ( ) Donation for Research

at: _____ cemetery

I have ( ) or have not ( ) consulted with the above named cemetery regarding: a cemetery plot ( )

a vault ( )   crypt ( )   niche for created remains ( )   memorial marker ( ) services and a casket ( )

The location or number of my burial plot (cemetery, mausoleum, columbarium niche) or other instructions is

_____ I

I do wish ( )   I do not wish ( )   or ( ) let my family decide to have an open casket at calling hours.

If open: Clothing _____ Jewelry _____ Glasses on ( ) off ( )